SPREAD

WINGS AND SOAR

AS A CHAMPION

MOTIVATIONAL AND INSPIRATIONAL QUOTES FOR TEENS, CHOSEN BY TEENS

Annette R. Pearson

Book Belongs To:

_____

_____

Listening To Your Voice Publishing

Empowering Transformations   www.ltyvpublishing.co.uk

to ms pearson.

" SPREAD YOUR

WINGS "

—set 3.

Dedication and Acknowledgement

This book is dedicated to the students I have taught at ATAM Academy London, especially my form group and science students who are now in the class of 2024.

This book would not have been so special without the motivational and inspirational quotes you wanted to write on the whiteboard in my classroom to share with others.

I promised to place them in a book for you before you leave secondary school, so here it is.

I want you to know that you are a fantastic group of students with so much talent and potential. You are the reason why many staff members enjoy teaching at the school.

As a couple of you wrote on my whiteboard two years ago, now is the time for us all to spread our wings and not just fly but soar.

Why are Inspirational and Motivational Quotes Great for Teens?

I know the last couple of years have impacted your mental health and well-being in so many ways. First, it was the pandemic, and now it is the cost-of-living crisis and other global challenges.

Due to fearful internal thoughts, many of you have lost your voice and the art of effectively communicating face-to-face.

As I spoke with my students and other teens, one thing became clear: they needed more than academic learning. They needed to learn ways to connect to their inner self and voice and express themselves in a way understood by each other and adults, including their parents or carers.

I hope you will be inspired, to write your own quotes, as you read this book, as they and I have been as we have gone on this personal development journey.

How to use this book?

There are two types of learners – passive and active.

Passive learners take information from others and use it in a limited way.

Active learners take the same information and internalise it and use it in many ways.

In this book, you are going to find a collection of quotes. You will see there is space for you to write your own quotes and thoughts on different pages in the book.

The best way to get the most out of this book will be to complete the different exercises, but the choice is yours.

I hope you will spread your wings and soar like an eagle high in the sky.

Ms Pearson

"Listen to your inner voice, and do not let anyone stop you from being the person you know, within, you need to be."

Ruth Pearson

"Your legacy is every life you've touched."

Maya Angelou

What is your legacy?

"No F.O.C.U.S! No Progress."

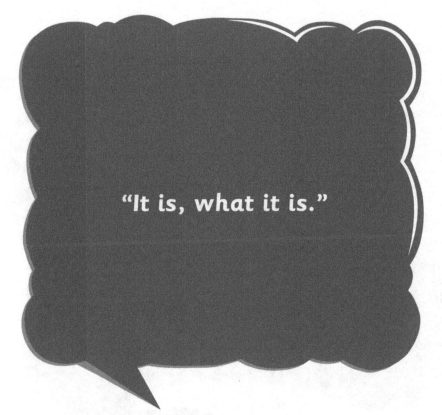

"It is, what it is."

Chosen by
Kareena

Everything happens for a reason.

"Believe in yourself."

"Don't let your difficulty become your identity."

"Expectation is a mindset."

"Everything created starts as a thought."

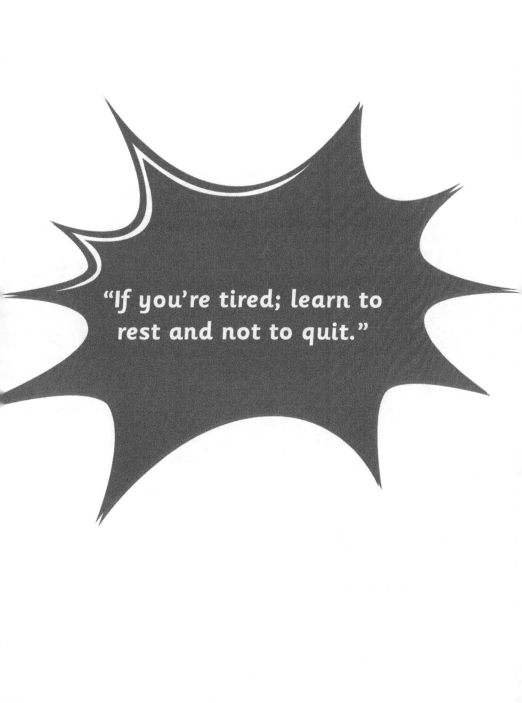

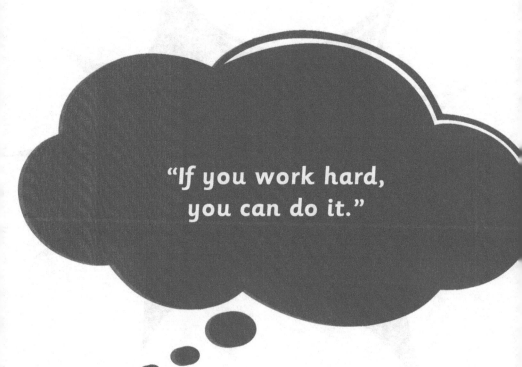

"If you work hard,
you can do it."

Chosen by
Trisha

"The actions you do today will come back to you in the future."

Write your own quote below!

"The best is yet to come."

Chosen by
Sanjana

"Choose the battles to fight, and the ones to walk away from."

Chosen by
Ms Pearson

Where are you heading to?

"Life goes on."

Chosen by
Devpal

"You are enough!"

Chosen by
Ramla

"Success is final. Failure is not fatal. It is the courage to continue that counts."

Chosen by Ravinder

"Never give up because
if you do, you will
never get far."

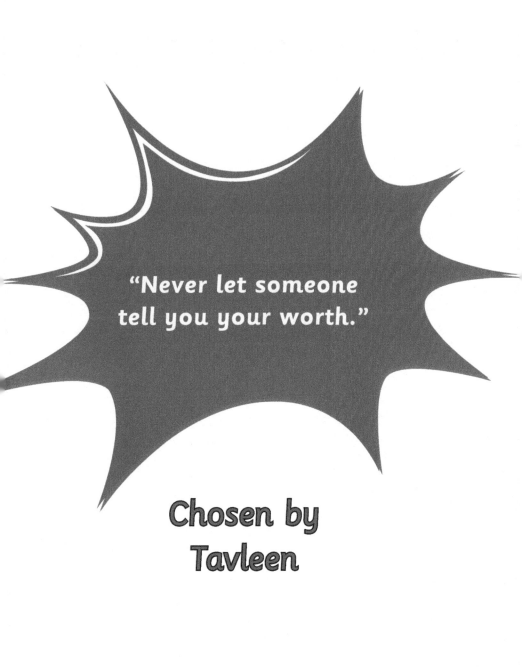

What are you worth?

"Be yourself as long as you're not a horrible person."

Chosen by Abjot

What words are you using to describe yourself?

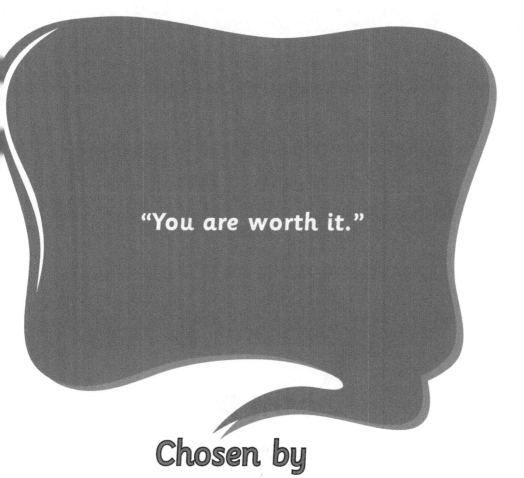

"You are worth it."

Chosen by
Tavleen

"Focus on the positives
instead of the negatives."

Chosen by
Jae

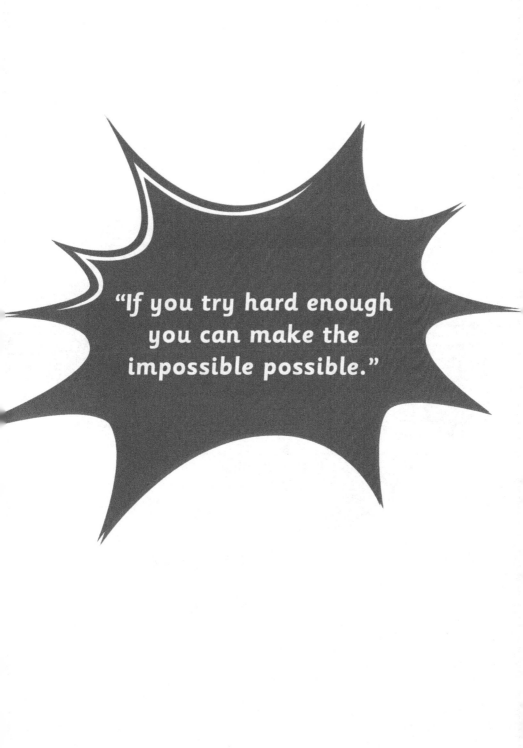

"No sacrifice is too great."

Chosen by
Faiaz

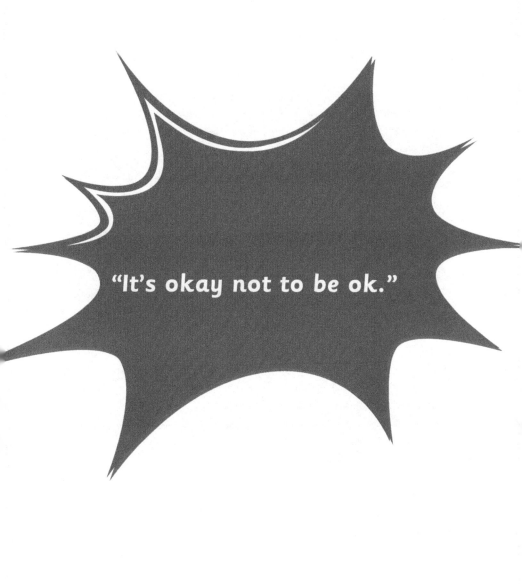

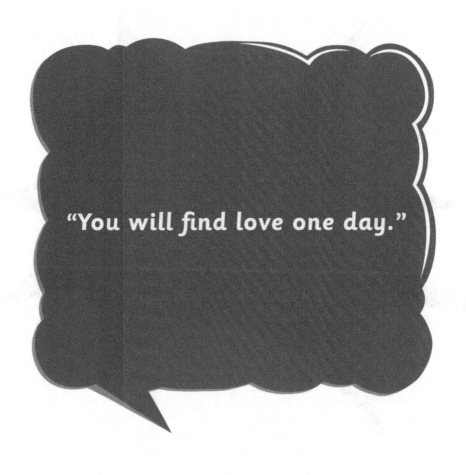

"People will always have some sort of opinion. Stop caring and live your own life."

Chosen by
Japji

"You make a big difference in someone's life."

Chosen by Harpreet

"Why are you changing
yourself for others?"

Chosen by
Japji

"You are wonderful, fantastic, pretty, lovely, amazing, nice, beautiful, cool and great."

Chosen by
Harpreet

What words can you use to describe yourself?

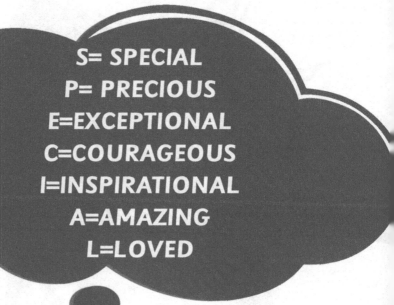

S= SPECIAL
P= PRECIOUS
E=EXCEPTIONAL
C=COURAGEOUS
I=INSPIRATIONAL
A=AMAZING
L=LOVED

Ms Pearson

Write your own meaning below.

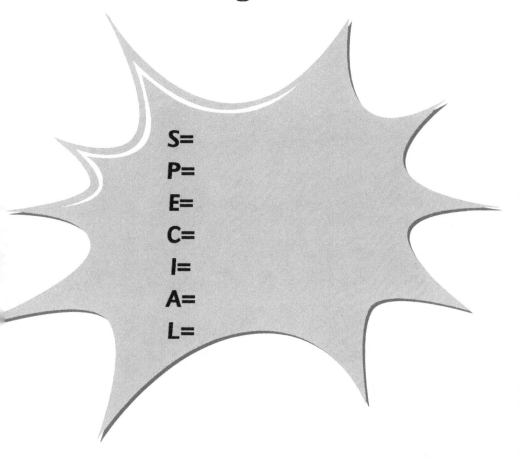

S=
P=
E=
C=
I=
A=
L=

"Don't change yourself
for other people."

Chosen by
Kareena

"You look alright."

Chosen by
Sienna

"You may be funny."

Chosen by
Sienna

"Don't let negative thoughts get to your head."

Chosen by Kareena

"Remember you need the bad days to make the good days better."

Chosen by Kareena

Describe the day you are having today.

What project are you working on at the moment?

Write your quote below

"Don't let someone stop you from being yourself."

"Don't let others define yourself."

"Revenge is a fools' game."

Chosen by
Faiaz

"Even if you get knocked down, you can still stand back up."

Chosen by
Ishmail

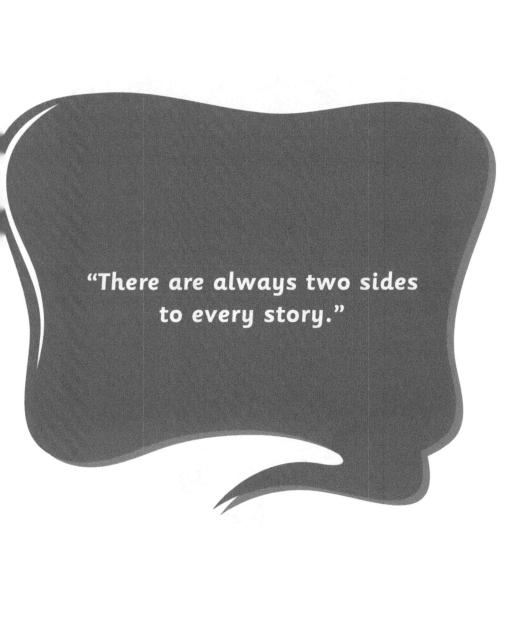

"There are always two sides to every story."

"Keep calm, and
do what's best."

Chosen by
Isher

Write your quote below

"Success is not a choice;
it is a process."

"Keep going, because you will find at the end of the day it was worth it."

"You can't spell impossible, without possible."

Chosen by Ramla

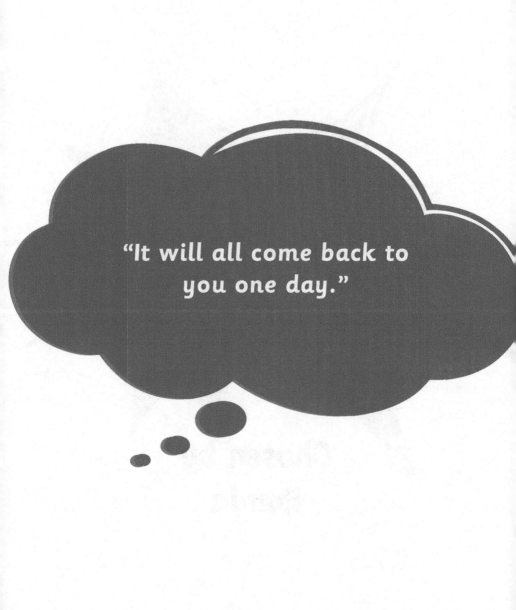

Write your quote below

"If someone says to you, "You are stupid", do not believe them."

"Never give up! Remember it was the tortoise which won the race, not the hare."

Ms Pearson

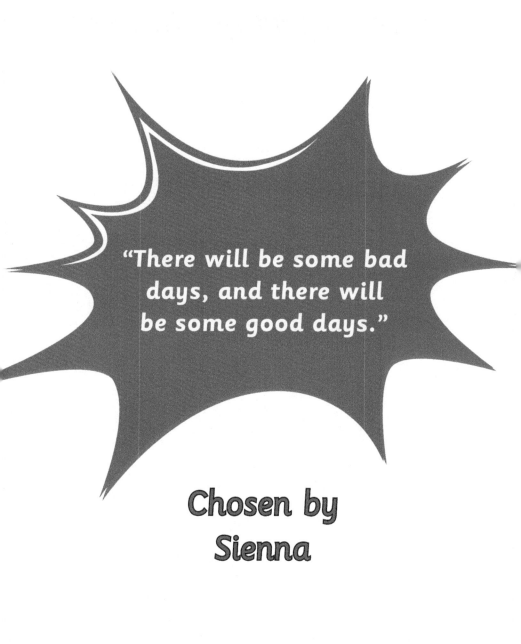

Write your quote here

Write your quote here

"If someone asks you, "What do you want to do with your life in 10-year life?" reply, "I'm not waiting for 10 years, I'm starting now!""

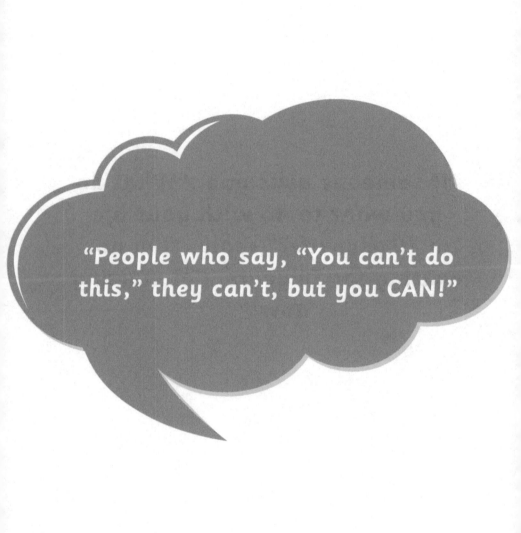

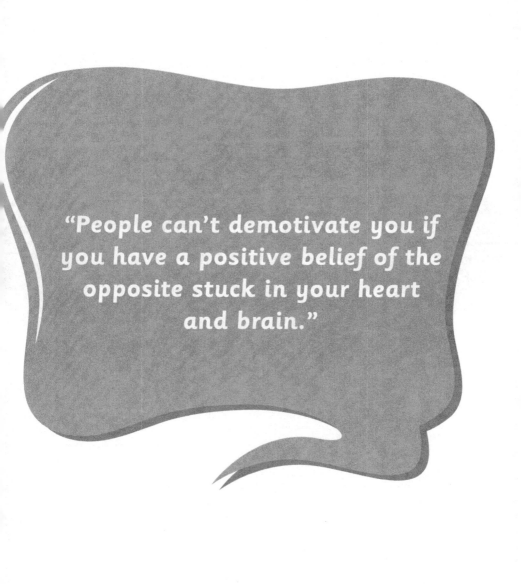

"People can't demotivate you if you have a positive belief of the opposite stuck in your heart and brain."

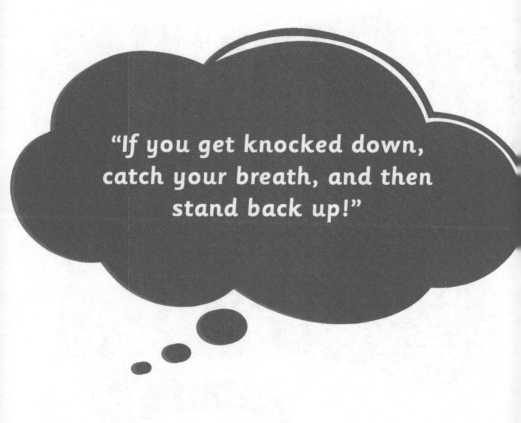

Write your quote here

"Keep calm, and be yourself."

Chosen by
Isher

"Failure is the first step
to success."

"The only way to do great work
is to love what you do."

Chosen by
Simran

"Be grateful for everything you have."

Chosen by
Ishkeerat

List three things you are grateful for today.

Write your quote here

"Actions, always speak louder than words."

Chosen by
Ishkeerat

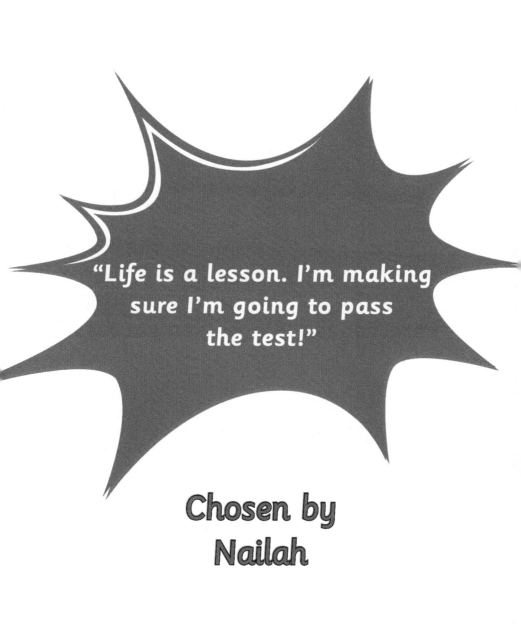

"Forgiveness is a key to success."

"The actions you put into your work will always come back to you."

Chosen by Manpreet

Write Your Quote Below

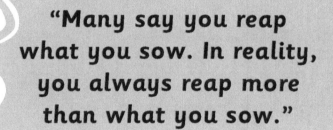

"Many say you reap what you sow. In reality, you always reap more than what you sow."

Ms Pearson

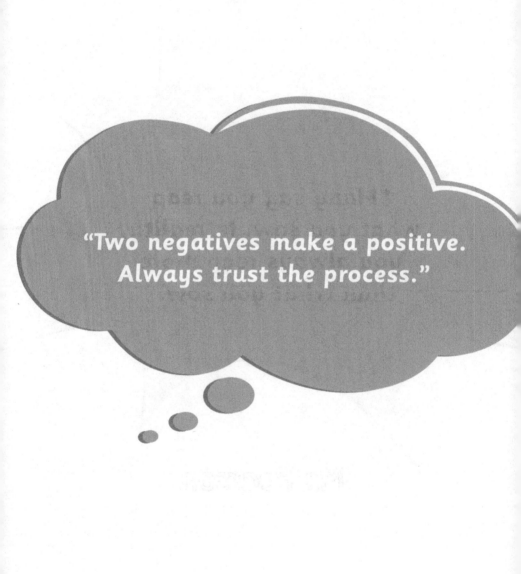

"Never give up! I'll say it again, NEVER GIVE UP!"

Chosen by
Manvinder

What is something you are finding hard?
What is the first small step you can take to achieve your goal?

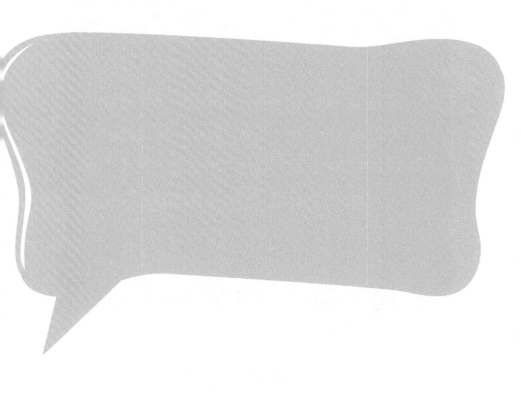

"Live as if you were to die tomorrow. So, forget the challenges of the past and live your best life today."

Chosen by
Ranvir

What is one special thing you are going to do today?

Write your thoughts below...

"Others may judge you from the outside, and may not say good things about you. But don't take on their beliefs because deep within, you know who you really are."

"When your alarm goes off in the morning you have two choices. Go back to sleep and carry on dreaming, or wake up and chase those dreams."

What dreams are you going to chase today?

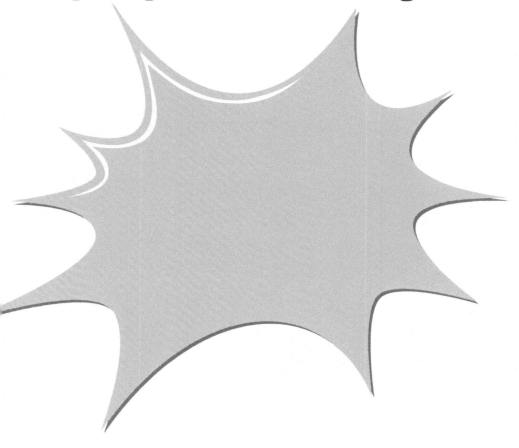

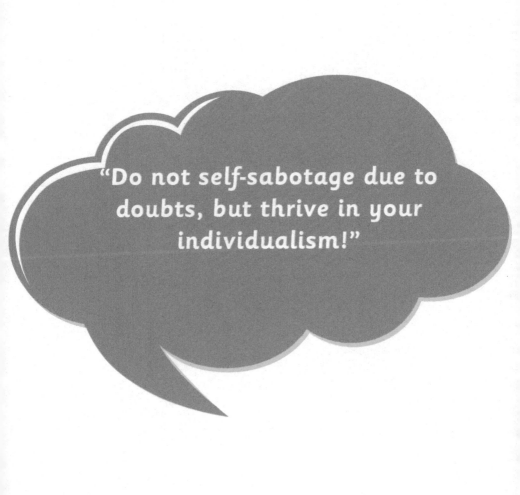

What makes you thrive?

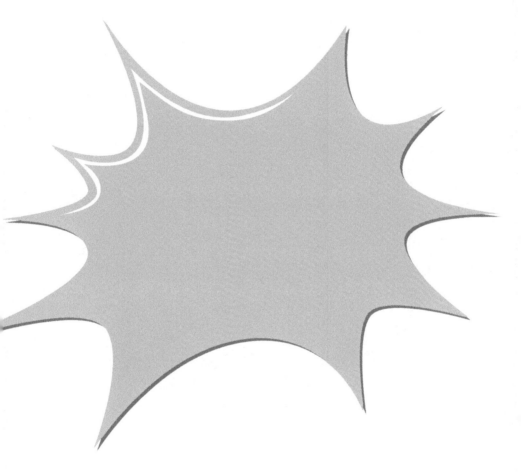

"Thank you for using
this journal.
I hope you too have been
inspired and motivated!"

Your Final Thoughts

Annette Ruth Pearson has taught in the education sector for over 35 years, mainly in the secondary sector. She has held many senior and middle leadership roles.

Her work extends beyond the classroom, as she has collaborated with numerous youth and adult voluntary organisations, serving as a counsellor, mediator, and mental health ambassador. Her efforts have not only brought out hidden greatness but also transformed lives.

At Atam Academy, she is using her skills as a Careers and Wellbeing Leader.

If you would like to contact her, she can be reached at

info@ltyvpublishing.co.uk

If you have enjoyed reading this book, please remember to leave us a review.

Thank you

Made in the USA
Monee, IL
01 October 2024

66984092R00066